RECOGNISING

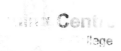

Michael Rose is Director of Reward and Recognition at Aon, based in London. He has held a number of other senior corporate HR roles and has over 10 years' experience as an HR consultant, most recently with Arthur Andersen. As a consultant Michael worked with public- and private-sector clients, both in the UK and abroad, helping to develop effective reward and recognition programmes. He holds an MA in HR Management, is a Fellow of the CIPD and an Associate of the Chartered Insurance Institute. Michael writes and speaks extensively on reward and recognition and associated HR issues.

RECOGNISING PERFORMANCE

NON-CASH REWARDS

MICHAEL ROSE

CHARTERED INSTITUTE OF PERSONNEL AND DEVELOPMENT

For Roslyn

First published in 2001

Design and typesetting by
Wyvern 21, Bristol

Printed in Great Britain by
the Short Run Press, Exeter

British Library Cataloguing-in-Publication Data
A catalogue record for this book is available
from the British Library

ISBN 0-85292-921-8

Chartered Institute of Personnel and Development, CIPD House,
Camp Road, Wimbledon, London SW19 4UX
Tel: 020-8971-9000   Fax: 020-8263-3333
E-mail: cipd@cipd.co.uk
Website: www.cipd.co.uk
Incorporated by Royal Charter. Registered charity no. 1079797.

Contents

Acknowledgements

I would like to acknowledge Larraine Gooch of Oxford Brookes University for her support in the original research from which this book grew; Arthur Andersen Human Capital Practice for their assistance and support in undertaking the unpublished survey of recognition practice in major companies (the author's survey); and Thames Water and British Airways for allowing information on their recognition programmes to be quoted freely.

Introduction

In 1994, a major UK bank undertook an attitude survey in one of its divisions and found that, above all else, *the* most significant cause of motivation problems was a lack of simple day-to-day recognition – acknowledgement or appreciation of what people do. A 1999 survey of managers throughout industry found that lack of recognition was cited by two-thirds of respondents as the main factor that would prompt them to hand in their notice (Roffey Park Management Institute 1999).

As these two examples suggest (more evidence is given in Chapter 1), lack of effective recognition, which is common in many organisations, can be an important cause of demotivation and staff turnover. In these highly competitive times, where recruitment and retention are the main concern for many organisations, we need to ensure that we are maximising our chances of keeping well-motivated people in our organisation.

This book aims to show how to develop simple non-cash programmes that can have a huge impact on motivation and retention at a very low cost – what we will call 'recognition programmes'. Effective recognition programmes can be anything from simple day-to-day thanks through to major corporate initiatives. In the following chapters we discuss the range of programmes available, and how you can maximise the opportunities and avoid the pitfalls in their design and use.

1

Why is recognition important?

- ✔ Recognition defined
- ✔ How recognition can make an impact
- ✔ Who says recognition is important?
    Needs theory – Reinforcement theory – Current writers
- ✔ Evidence for the importance of recognition

Recognition defined

This book is a practical guide on how to develop, design and establish programmes to promote and support recognition within an organisation. First it is useful to understand what recognition is and why it is important.

Hale and Maehling (1993) define recognition as 'a broad, all-encompassing process that boosts employee self-esteem and builds an environment of trust, respect, and independence throughout the company. [It] can be formal, informal, or day-to-day...[it] is an action or activity, and as such, it is non-monetary.'

Pitts (1995) sees recognition as 'the demonstration of appreciation for a level of performance, an achievement or a contribution to an objective. It can be confidential or public, casual or formal. It is always in addition to pay. In general terms, reward is the pay and recognition is the handshake.'

How recognition can make an impact

A number of examples will be used throughout this book, but before we begin let us see how some organisations have used recognition programmes. The first example shows how a recognition programme can support the introduction of values.

Thames Water has defined core values for the business that it sees as important both for customers and employees – known as Values in Practice (VIP). As part of the values work, a recognition programme was introduced where anyone could nominate anyone else who displayed the values in action. This programme has been used as one of the ways of keeping values 'on the agenda'. It is high profile and is well publicised and uses the individuals who are recognised in the programme as role models illustrating the key values.

The second example is a programme that supports customer service and improving management styles.

British Airways developed its initial recognition programme, for customer-facing staff, to reinforce the emphasis on customer care. Its programmes have been developed over time and are now brought together under the umbrella of 'BRAVO'. This approach to recognition goes from the informal 'thank you' to small-value BRAVO awards, 'Awards for Excellence' and the quarterly Premier Awards. The BRAVO programme provides flexible guidance to managers on how and when to 'recognise' people and suggests appropriate forms of recognition.

The third example is a programme that integrates recognition with a number of other behaviours.

Based on evidence from a staff attitude survey, a retail pub chain developed an integrated programme to help improve communications and poor recognition of people. The programme allowed people to receive points that could be spent from a 'gift catalogue'. Points could be accumulated in a number of ways, such as by managers using a points 'cheque book' to recognise any example of excellent customer service. They could also be received for making relevant suggestions to improve customer service or processes and acquiring NVQs. The scheme was piloted using a control group. Where the scheme was used there was a very significant increase in sales, profit and customer attitude scores over the control group.

Who says recognition is important?

Needs theory

In 1936 Carnegie emphasised that the single most crucial factor in dealing with people was to recognise their desire for a feeling of importance. Hertzberg and Maslow both found recognition to be central to their models of motivation.

Hertzberg's famous theory states that there are:

- motivators relating to job *content* that can change behaviour positively: achievement, recognition (which could come from almost anyone – supervisor, client, peer, etc), work itself, responsibility and advancement
- 'hygiene factors', relating to job *context*, which act as dissatisfiers: company policy and administration, supervision, salary, interpersonal relations and working conditions; although these are commonly the main source of dissatisfaction, they do not become a source of motivation if 'reversed'.

After achievement, recognition was the second most frequent factor (motivator) related to positive feelings about the job. The lack of recognition for work done was also a very significant factor for negative feelings about the job. The research found that whereas achievement on its own can be a source of good feelings about the job, recognition is rarely independent of achievement. 'A feeling that you have achieved and a feeling that you have been recognised are the two most frequent feelings that are associated with an increase in job satisfaction' (Hertzberg *et al* 1959).

4

Hertzberg concludes that the act of recognition, which is not related to a specific sense of achievement, becomes a fairly trivial factor. This finding is a core consideration for when we look at designing recognition programmes. It is valueless to develop a programme that does not encourage recognition of real achievement.

Maslow (1970) saw motivation in terms of a hierarchy of needs moving from basic physiological and safety needs through the need for belonging and love to the need for esteem and ultimately self-actualisation. It is only when a lower order need has been satisfied that a need higher up the hierarchy may become a cause of motivation.

Maslow's 'esteem' need is essentially a combination of two elements:

- self-respect or self-esteem, which he sees as 'the desire for strength, for achievement, for adequacy, for mastery and competence, for confidence in the face of the world and for independence and freedom'
- the esteem (or recognition) of others, 'what we may call the desire for reputation or prestige (defining it as respect or esteem from other people), status, fame and glory, dominance, recognition, attention importance, dignity or appreciation'.

Pay and recognition may be viewed as part of a (Maslow's) hierarchy, where pay satisfies basic needs and recognition forms a part of the higher-order esteem needs.

As Armstrong (1996) argues, recognition needs are linked with the esteem needs in Maslow's hierarchy. Goddard (1987) also says that 'self-esteem results from personal recognition'. This combination of self-esteem and esteem through others is a vital element in the motivational model.

Reinforcement theory

Recognition can also be a factor in reinforcing behaviour.

Skinner developed the model of 'operant conditioning' from work on animals. He found that an animal that was rewarded by food as a consequence of its voluntary action (for example nudging a lever) tended to repeat the behaviour. This positive reinforcement was at the core of Skinner's operant theory of motivation (Skinner 1953, quoted in Steers and Porter 1991).

The opposite of positive reinforcement is 'extinction', where a behaviour that is not reinforced decreases and eventually disappears (although behaviour can be maintained easily when only an occasional response is reinforced). Further work found that intermittent rather than continuous reinforcement actually increases the desired responses; that is, rewards that are given too frequently may diminish motivation (La Motta 1995). This may suggest that the value of recognition diminishes if used excessively.

Current writers

Many current management writers see recognition as an important, sometimes vital, aspect of motivating people at work.

Ed Lawler says that 'people respond to something that costs little or nothing, and that something is called recognition' (quoted in Hale and Maehling 1993).

Blanchard and Johnson (1993) emphasise the importance of recognition to counter the common management attitude of being quick to criticise failure but slow to praise success. They say that managers should 'catch people doing something right'.

Pitts (1995) says that recognition is 'the demonstration by human beings that they have noticed and appreciated the actions, achievements and contribution of others. It is fundamental to humans being at ease with themselves, because it is thus that our very purpose is characterised, worthy or unworthy.'

Coming right up to date, Lyons (2000) argues that there are seven core leadership skills that are vital for today's leaders in the post-factory setting. One of the essential seven is 'giving recognition':

> This is a powerful leadership activity that is not emphasised enough in traditional management styles, and is a key to making strategy work over time. The results that come from appropriate recognition of a job well done are extremely positive and motivational to both the individual and the team. Giving recognition can also be one of the easiest skills to coach.

Evidence for the importance of recognition

- In a study by the American Productivity and Quality Centre, 91 per cent of employees were found to value recognition above other remuneration (quoted in La Motta 1995).
- A research project covering 5,000 employees at all levels found that 70 per cent wanted specific individual recognition for a job well done (Wall and Jeffries, quoted in Hale and Maehling 1993).

- A survey of 1,500 employees found that the number-one workplace motivator was recognition. Specifically, the top motivator was personal congratulations from the manager for a job well done, which should be immediate and specific (Caudron 1995).
- A study by Blessing/White of Voluntary Effort in the Work Force, quoted in Managing Customer Service (1998), identified the main factors that motivated the employees in the study; recognition was placed fourth, after responsibility for one's work, a sense of worth and a job that makes good use of skills.

Much of this evidence comes from research undertaken in the USA. Certainly, the 'recognition industry' is much more developed there than in the UK – evidence suggests, however, that even though the approach may be different, the need for recognition is similar.

In a survey by International Survey Research reported in Syedain (1995), the first three job priorities for UK workers were: being treated with fairness and respect, job security and recognition for good performance. Seventy per cent of people said that recognition was 'very important', but only 37 per cent were satisfied with the recognition they got. This was the widest discrepancy among the 12 job priorities polled.

Recognition is an important and enduring element in motivating people at work. So the real question is: how can we use recognition to improve the motivation and retention of people in the organisation? The rest of this book tries to answer this question.

What are recognition programmes?

- ☑ Definition
- ☑ How recognition programmes are used

Definition

The author's definition of a recognition programme is:

> Typically, a non-cash award given to employees in recognition of a high level of accomplishment or performance, such as customer care or support to colleagues, which is not dependent on achievement against a given target. It may be local and immediate, such as a voucher given by a supervisor, or more formal and high profile, such as employee of the month.

There are three core elements in this definition:

● Although some recognition programmes use cash, good practice is to use some form of tangible non-cash award, which is likely to be much more effective for the purpose. One reason is so that the recognition is emphasised, not the payment; other reasons are discussed in Chapter 4.

- A true recognition programme is not dependent on achievement of a predetermined target. Such a scheme would be an incentive or performance-related pay programme; these have their place but are not the subject of this book.
- Third, recognition programmes are not all high-profile corporate initiatives; they can be very low-key local events. In fact, it is best to think of them as a continuum.

Local, informal, low key, simple	Corporate, formal, high profile

Many companies develop a series of recognition pro-grammes to try and spread recognition throughout the company. For example, Tennant in the USA developed its 'three-dimensional model': formal recognition, informal recognition and day-to-day recognition (Hale and Maehling 1993).

How recognition programmes are used

We have seen from the examples in Chapter 1 that pro-grammes will vary from one organisation to another. What a particular organisation may value and the format it uses to recognise it will depend on its aims and culture. What is common is that the programmes are separate from pay and that they encourage the recognition of people doing something that is valued by the organisation.

A common use of recognition programmes is to support managers and encourage the simple acknowledgement of the good things people do. So a recognition programme can be an important part of the 'kit bag' of processes and interventions available to managers.

However, recognition should be something more than just an occasional practice, but 'an all-pervading attitude that people can count on' (La Motta 1995). This integration of recognition into the organisation contrasts with the typically formal and centrally controlled pay system.

It is the whole person who comes to work and it is the totality of work that affects people. So it is important to think how recognition programmes relate to other HR programmes and how the different programmes can work together. For example, what messages do the existing pay programmes carry? If there is a link to performance, how does it work? What style and elements of leadership are promoted in management development and training programmes? These issues are discussed in Chapter 3.

3

How do recognition programmes fit with other HR programmes?

☑ Recognition and the relationship with reward
☑ Recognition and performance management
☑ Recognition and development and training
☑ Role of HR and line management

Recognition and the relationship with reward

The relationship between recognition and reward is complex. However, Juran, quoted in La Motta (1995), explains it well:

- Recognition is typically non-financial and consists of 'ceremonial' actions taken to publicise meritorious performance.
- Rewards are salary increases, bonuses and promotions keyed to job performance and usually conferred in private, primarily focusing on conduct of operations using performance appraisal or merit ratings.

Of course rewards can carry important messages. Tyson (1995) considers that there are strong symbolic overtones within organisational rewards: 'Monetary rewards may not motivate in the long term, but they certainly symbolise the value corporations attach to specific behaviours – for example rewarding long service, interpreted as loyalty, or rewarding performance above other attributes.' So if you want to see what an organisation truly values, look at what it actually pays for – not what it says.

There is sometimes confusion between recognition and incentives. Non-cash recognition programmes should be contrasted with incentive plans such as bonuses. Recognition programmes are not incentive plans. They seek to change behaviour by reinforcing positive actions – they do not do so by using the incentive of a carrot. An incentive plan carries the message: 'You do that and I will give you this.' A recognition programme, on the other hand, seeks to reinforce the great things people are already doing.

Many managers have deeply held assumptions about the role of incentive pay in motivation. This can be because money is the only 'currency' used by some organisations to thank people, giving the message that it is only cash that demonstrates your worth (Nelson 1996). In other words, these managers promote a self-fulfilling prophecy so that employees learn to expect cash as the only true form of thanks. If a child is deprived of love by its parents but receives only toys, then although it may crave the love it ends up demanding more toys – the currency that the parent uses. The parallel with reward and recognition is clear – what is really needed is genuine appreciation and understanding by managers of employees. However, as with children – toys are better than nothing at all (La Motta

1995). Non-financial recognition programmes can help to shift the balance back to real thanks and appreciation and so complement the pay system. This is discussed in more detail in Chapter 4.

British Airways simply but effectively differentiates as follows:

● Reward – is about pay or compensation
● Incentives – are about meeting targets
● Recognition – is about saying 'thank you'.

Recognition and performance management

Performance management systems often underpin performance-related pay. The challenge lies in developing a system that allows the effective translation of performance into pay. A survey by William M. Mercer of companies' performance-related pay systems discovered that 47 per cent of companies reported that their employees 'found the systems neither fair nor sensible'. Fifty-one per cent said that the performance management system provided little value to the company (Pfeffer 1998).

A classic approach to performance management is to use some form of annual objectives-based system, where performance is reviewed against the objectives set. However, objectives and performance criteria can be very difficult to set, in particular where the organisation changes rapidly and there are no tangible outputs (Legge 1995). The individual is often rewarded for achievement against so-called 'SMART' objectives. However, the emphasis on measurability can lead to objectives being selected because they can be easily measured rather than because they add value. Recognition programmes, on the other hand, do not try to incentivise people to achieve specific objectives, but celebrate and reinforce the great things people do (Rose 2000).

Although a key value in an appraisal-driven performance management system is 'no surprises' (ie at the annual review, because there should have been constant feedback throughout the year), in reality this is rarely the case. The annual cycle of performance and pay review provides limited opportunities for line managers to give more regular feedback and recognition. Much more regular recognition opportunities need to be part of the whole process (Hale and Maehling 1993). A non-financial recognition programme can be designed to promote the recognition of the positive things people do throughout the year and so can sit alongside the performance management process. Where someone has received some kind of recognition award it should be referred to in the performance management discussions. If recognising people is an important value in the organisation then managers should have their performance in effectively recognising people as a factor in their own appraisal.

Recognition and development and training

Non-financial recognition programmes are often introduced to help change people management behaviour and the interaction of people in an organisation; they may be part of a larger cultural change programme. Recognition needs to be defined in terms that the organisation will understand and will find useful and then should form part of a greater whole, not just stand on its own in the recognition programme. If one of the organisation's values is to recognise people, then this needs to be reinforced, not only through the non-financial recognition programme itself, but also in the training and development of the people who will operate it.

The Thames Water programme was introduced as part of the development of values in the business. Three interrelated elements were at the core of bringing the values to life: leadership, communications and people. The recognition programme supported the values in that it encouraged people formally to recognise values in action. But as part of the same values work there was considerable briefing and training of the values proposition of which the recognition was part.

Development and training should help drive the message of the importance and role of recognition in the motivation and management of people. Recognition programmes and training and development need to reinforce similar behaviours in a consistent and coherent way.

British Airways sees recognition as an important part of any manager's job. It uses six core 'management capabilities' to demonstrate what good management should look like. Each capability is broken down into component elements. For example, 'managing performance' breaks down to four elements – delegating effectively, performance management, coaching and developing others, and motivating others. It is in 'motivating others' that thanking, recognising and valuing people and celebrating success feature. The management capabilities are at the core of management training and development within which the manager's role in recognising people is covered.

Promotion may bring further intrinsic reward to the extent that the new job offers greater challenge, opportunity and recognition. However, the motivational effect of promotion may only be sustained for a relatively short period so, although promotion may play a part, it is questionable when used as the key means to recognise and reward performance (Pitts 1995). Also, with flatter organisational structures and an increase in broadbanding – 20 per cent of companies have broadbanding and another 17 per cent will be introducing it (CBI/Hay 1995) – the opportunities for conventional promotions have become more limited. Although recognition through a suitable programme should not be a substitute for promotion and development, it can provide many more opportunities to recognise people in less formal but still significant and valued ways.

Role of HR and line management

The relative roles of HR and line management in recognition will depend on the way in which they work together on existing people-related issues. Typically, though HR will develop the recognition programmes in conjunction with line management, the actual 'recognition' is likely to be initiated by line managers, co-workers or customers. This really needs to be the sort of HR programme that is owned by the line managers. If it becomes seen as another HR project then it is unlikely to be successful. It is therefore important that HR professionals work with the line managers to develop the programme, getting buy-in as they do so.

How should you recognise people?

☑ Who will value recognition most?
☑ How to recognise people
    Informal thanks – How to do it – More formal approaches to recognition
☑ Financial versus non-financial awards
    Non-cash award ideas
☑ Creating winners not losers
☑ Teams or individuals
☑ Who should do the recognising?

Who will value recognition most?

Evidence presented in Chapter 1 shows how recognition can be a critical, and often missing, motivator for people at work. But recognition programmes may be particularly valuable for certain groups. For example, Tulgan (1996) argues that recognition is vital for managing and motivating the so-called 'Generation X'.

Hertzberg believed that recognition might be more important for more senior people in an organisation. However, the survey of various researchers' work he reports (1968) rather suggests that people occupying the least skilled and perhaps most undervalued jobs may particularly value recognition. The CEO of a residential maid service in the USA said that 'many of our workers have never known respect [so] getting it changes them for the better' (Maynard 1997). Roz Jeffries, President of Performance Enhancement Group Inc, a US HR consulting firm, says, 'People at the lower [wage] levels beg for the intangibles – the pat on the back, the verbal "thank you". Self-esteem is a little lower, and they want to know they're okay' (Maynard 1997).

It is more common to find recognition programmes in retail, hotel and catering, leisure, transport and service businesses, primarily because of the high customer interface. Such organisations frequently use non-financial recognition to support customer service.

> A retail pub chain introduced its programme based on the potential achievement of a range of individual and team aims and behaviours. For example – knowing 1,000 customers by name and their favourite drink; suggestions to improve some aspect of customer service or systems; any significant customer service (rewarded with spot awards); level of customer service based on a quarterly assessment from mystery visitor visits; acquisition of National Vocational Qualifications (NVQs) in a relevant catering subject.
>
> The catering industry has people in jobs commonly regarded as low value, potentially associated with low esteem. A central theme in this scheme is to find things for people to succeed at to build their own level of confidence and self-esteem. That is the philosophy of having a range of different things, each of which can provide points, including the acquisition of NVQs by people who otherwise had no qualifications of any kind.

We should also consider the recognition for the partner of the employee. When someone works late or unsociable hours, it is also the partner who suffers. After a heavy storm five male workers in a telephone company were sent out to do overnight repairs on Valentine's day. As a form of thanks, each employee's spouse was sent a box of chocolates with a card expressing the company's appreciation for her husband's efforts (Nelson 1994).

How to recognise people

Although this section considers direct awards as part of recognition, it is worth reflecting that people can feel recognised in many different ways. For many people, in particular top performers, increased responsibility and reduced supervision can be rewards in themselves. Alternatives may be additional time off or alternative assignments (Joinson 1996). Empowerment can be a form of recognition to the extent that the individual is being given the tools and authority to achieve results. Empowerment requires a sense of trust and implies that the individual's competence is recognised and appreciated.

There are different 'levels' of recognition from very informal local individual initiatives – the manager saying 'thank you' – to very formal corporate programmes. Armstrong (1996) sees that 'recognition is also provided by managers who listen to and act upon suggestions of their team members and, importantly, acknowledge their contribution'. Johnson and Redmond (1998) believe that 'a sense of recognition comes about when people are called by their names, when their opinion is valued and their queries or comments are treated seriously'.

Informal thanks

A study of 800 healthcare workers by McCormick and Ilgen, quoted in La Motta (1995), sought to identify the motivational impact of each of a number of recognition techniques using a four-quadrant model for analysis, as shown below.

	Company-initiated	Manager-initiated
Performance		*Most motivating*
Presence	*Least motivating*	

The study found that the most motivating techniques were manager-initiated and related to performance. The least motivating related to recognition of presence (such as a birthday card), particularly when company-initiated. Although the centrally produced birthday card may be efficient, it is not effective. This reinforces Hertzberg's view that recognition is only of value when associated with achievement.

Nelson quotes a study of 1,500 employees that found personal oral congratulations and a personal note from the manager were the top two out of 67 potential incentives he evaluated.

How to do it

Whether orally or in writing:

- be personal – use the person's name

- make it specific – refer to exactly what the person did
- be clear – explain why it is appreciated
- make it public.

La Motta (1995) emphasises the need to acknowledge individuals uniquely. She argues that much of the recognition employed by managers is in a form that they themselves would value, not necessarily what the recipient would appreciate. It is therefore important to understand first what makes us feel recognised. La Motta suggests that we really need to know how individuals operate to be able to decide what form any recognition should take. For example, introverted people may gain maximum reward from knowing they have done a good job, whereas extrovert types may require the recognition of others.

Harvey-Jones (1994) believes that 'the art of the unscheduled reward lies in the personalisation of the reward and the manner of its giving, as much as its cash value'. He adds that:

> Unscheduled rewards must be presented in ways which are public and overt. The fact that unscheduled rewards are made is in itself a message to all your people that you as a manager and the company as an organisation are interested in individuals and individual performance, that you are close to what is going on, that it is appreciated and that this appreciation can take a tangible form.

More formal approaches to recognition

In addition to recognising people by an oral or written 'thank you', you should also consider more formal approaches. These are likely to have a more structured (but fun) setting and to include some publicity about what people have done to receive the award:

- The next step up from simple one-to-one recognition is formally to present an individual with a recognition award at an existing event, such as a department meeting, training or briefing session.
- To raise the profile some more, lay on a special local event such as a buffet lunch, where the individual is presented with the award.
- A corporate award programme may have a regular award ceremony – typically with lunch or dinner – where the winners are presented with their awards. This is often done by a senior person in the organisation – ideally the chief executive. The people to be awarded are often able to invite some guests to the event, such as family or work colleagues.

In each case you need to ensure an atmosphere of celebration. Southwest Airlines follows a number of common sense guidelines that contribute to the success of celebrations in the company (Freiberg and Freiberg 1996):

1 The celebration must be authentic – it must come from the heart.
2 The celebration must raise people's dignity and self-respect – it must never harm.
3 The celebration must be done right – it should be well co-ordinated, well timed and well executed in a quality way.

4 The celebration must appeal to the senses – use balloons, banners, flags, costumes, videos and photographs.

5 The celebration must be seen as an investment – it should not be seen as a cost.

6 The celebration must be cost-effective – look for the least expensive way to do it right.

Southwest's success in recognition can be summarised as follows:

- say 'thank you' often
- always celebrate people from the heart
- make heroes and heroines of employees who glorify your company's values
- find people who serve behind the scenes and celebrate their contributions
- create a celebration signature – balloons, photos, trophies
- celebrate at work like you do at home; celebrate at home like Southwest does at work.

Financial versus non-financial awards

Cash has the advantage of being easy to administer – every organisation already has a payroll, so why not just use it?

A recognition programme is not a substitute for pay. What is important is the recognition itself, not the financial or non-financial award. Where awards are paid in cash, particularly through the payroll, they tend to be seen by managers as part of pay. The more fundamental motivator – recognition of achievement – can get lost.

The author was working with an organisation reviewing its recognition programme. It paid recognition awards in the payroll, usually a month or more after the event. Tax was deducted and the payment was quickly used up in the regular monthly outgoings. Other than a letter informing the individual of the award, there was little or no celebration. Interviews and focus groups with managers showed that the dominant view was that this was really just part of the pay system; managers felt that the important part of the process was the pay. The great majority of recipients, on the other hand, said that the most memorable and important part was receiving the letter of thanks telling them they were getting an award.

There are a number of advantages of non-financial awards over cash:

- Non-financial awards differentiate the recognition programme from pay.
- Non-financial awards can have 'memory value' – that is, their effect is longer lasting. Every time the item is used or enjoyed the recipient may remember why and how he or she earned it (Gryna 1992; Brooks 1994). Although someone is unlikely to show his or her neighbour the pay slip, it is rather more acceptable to show off something tangible that has been earned. It is sometimes said that cash is a motivator for as long as it takes before it is spent.
- The perceived value of a non-financial award can be much higher than the actual cost, so that a

non-financial award is valued more highly than
cash of the same value (Brooks 1994).

- A non-financial award can be tailored to the needs
  and interests of the recipient, showing a greater
  amount of thought than a simple cash sum would
  reflect.

The three featured case studies each use a different approach to
awards:

- British Airways uses informal thanks, non-financial
  gifts, certificates signed by the CEO and luxury travel.
- Thames Water uses informal thanks, a letter signed by
  the CEO and a cash award of £1,000 for the winners.
  Although cash is generally not best practice, this is
  presented in a celebratory ceremony as a (tax-paid)
  cheque so that the emphasis is clearly on the
  recognition.
- The retail pub chain uses points that people can
  accumulate for a range of things and that they can
  then use to pay for gifts from a catalogue.

John Harvey-Jones (1994), ex-chairman of ICI, believes in the
value of what he terms 'non-systematic immediate awards'.
He argues that an immediate award of a few hundred
pounds accompanied by appropriate thanks from the manager will have a much greater positive motivational effect
and will cost much less than a salary increase at the end of
the year. He also believes in the value of a tangible gift –
referring to his own practice of sending cases of wine to
people who have done something particularly meritorious:
'The essence of the reward is that it is a tangible way of

saying thank you that is not put forward by the personnel department.'

Choice of award is important. If the aim is to maximise the perceived value to the recipient, then it is important to offer as much choice as possible (Cline 1997). The size of any award must acknowledge the size of the deed. If awards are too small they may trivialise the behaviour; if they are too large they may cause a sense of unfairness (Flannery *et al* 1996). Any tangible component of recognition should be seen as worthy in the minds of the recipients, 'but it is also a symbol of recognition and has to be properly presented and delivered' (Bryant 1994).

Different types of recognition programme have quite different levels of award. The author undertook an unpublished survey of recognition programmes in major private-sector companies in 1998 (hereafter 'the author's 1998 survey') that found that they tended to cluster into two groups. One included all the low-value, fairly informal awards that could be given frequently. Most typically these were gifts, retail vouchers or dinner out with one's partner, at a value of £25 to £200. At the other extreme were the high-profile awards given annually. These were relatively high-value and were commonly a holiday, other trip overseas or prizes/vouchers worth up to £3,000.

If you still insist in paying recognition awards through the payroll, then at least use the message space on most pay slips for further congratulations.

Non-cash award ideas

The choice of award is limited only by your imagination. But it is important to think carefully about the award and the individual. A huge bunch of flowers may look great, but how do you get it home on a bus? – so send the person home in a taxi as well. A food hamper may be well received, but it could backfire if the recipient is a vegetarian. Here are a few ideas to get you thinking:

- plaques or certificates
- bottle of champagne
- basket of fruit
- food hamper
- house cleaning for a year
- car parking for six months
- the prime parking spot in the office car park for a month
- dinner out for two
- cinema vouchers
- points-based catalogue gifts
- personalised items
- a small number of shares or share options in the company
- Fridays off in June
- magazine subscription
- retail shopping vouchers
- charity donation.

Hemsath and Yerkes (1997) give their top-ten list of the most popular recognition gifts:

1 a mug (preferably with a cartoon)
2 t-shirts
3 dinner out (lunch and breakfast as well)
4 gift certificates
5 balloons (delivered to the person at the workplace)
6 tickets to a sports event

7 books
8 plaques and trophies
9 popcorn or fruit baskets
10 joke/funny gifts.

Creating winners not losers

An individual being recognised may be motivated, but will it have a positive or negative effect on the rest of the population? There is a danger that highly publicised recognition awards can be divisive in that people other than the winners feel like losers. McAdams (quoted in Joinson 1996) believes that the typical 'employee of the month' concept creates a winners and losers environment, which will mitigate against people working together as a team. It is better to make programmes achievement-based rather than time-bound, so that the number of winners is unlimited.

You really cannot limit recognition to a quota. In one organisation where a formal programme was introduced to recognise outstanding performers, feedback showed that employees felt that the programme did not recognise enough people often enough (Hale and Maehling 1993). Mary Kay Cosmetics (La Motta 1995) has a well-developed reward programme and is often seen as one of the top 100 most motivating US companies to work for. There is a large range of non-financial awards available, up to pink Cadillacs, which are presented at the annual awards ceremony. There is no limit to the number of people who can receive the awards, and therefore each person competes only with himself or herself and no others in the company.

Harvey-Jones (1994) says that 'one of the purposes of unscheduled rewards is to underscore public recognition in a way which passes a little bit of glory on to the individual who has won a reward'. Nelson (1996) says that recognition is not just for the person who performed well; it is also a message to other employees about the type of performance that gets noticed in an organisation. Kanter, quoted in Nelson (1996), says, 'To the rest of the organisation, recognition creates role models and heroes and communicates the standards: these are the kinds of things that constitute great performance around here.'

> Thames Water's recognition programme was introduced for just this reason. It sees the recognition programme as not just for recognising the individuals directly affected, but for emphasising, through regular publicity, what living the values looks like.

If it is not clear to people why an individual has been chosen for a formal award it can lead to dissatisfaction. In the absence of clear reasons people will be guided by their own perceptions of the person (Hale and Maehling 1993). Yet, according to Crosby (quoted in La Motta 1995), 'genuine recognition of performance is something people really appreciate. They will continue to support the [recognition] program, whether or not they, as individuals, participate in the awards.'

Fairness and acceptability are vital to a successful programme. It is, therefore, a challenge to ensure that awards only go to those individuals whose achievements are of such a magnitude that they are recognised by superiors, subordinates and peers. In such circumstances, although an individual may feel that he or she should have received an award, he or she will not quibble about someone else's award (Friedson 1985).

In reviewing an existing recognition programme the author came across a number of people who had received an award but were embarrassed about it because they felt that it was undeserved, in that they had done nothing special. On investigation it appeared that the (cash) awards were being used by managers as a form of pay rather than recognition, which had the result of devaluing the whole programme. This illustrates Hertzberg's view that recognition without achievement is trivial. One of the changes that was introduced to improve this programme was that a group of previous winners, along with a cross-section of people in the business, were used as the 'judging panel' for the higher level of award. The selection was thus made by people's colleagues rather than higher management.

For selection for the British Airways Premier Award the company uses a group made up of a cross-section of recognition representatives from throughout the company to select the quarterly winners. Simple selection criteria are used to maintain some consistency. Yet most Premier nominations arise from unique situations and decisions are made according to a subjective 'tingle down the spine' test.

Thames Water uses a cross-section of people from around the business to select the VIP winners. This group also includes previous VIP winners.

Abbey National uses a panel of 12 people from all levels around the company to decide on any awards.

At Harvester restaurants an independent team of assessors test restaurants and it is their assessment that produces the winning restaurants (Syedain 1995).

The US company Tennant has a range of awards in addition to the formal annual 'Award of Excellence'. Initially, only a third of those nominated received the top 'Award of Excellence', the remainder received a 'Special Recognition Award'. A review of the programme found, however, that people who received the lower-level award often felt like losers, which had a negative rather than positive effect. Subsequently the 'two-tier' system was abolished (Hale and Maehling 1993).

Teams or individuals

The author's 1998 survey found that 49 per cent of the programmes reported were designed for recognising either teams or individuals, 46 per cent for recognising individuals only, and 5 per cent were for teams only. However, a number of respondents said that in practice awards are mostly given to individuals and not teams.

Recognition can be used to celebrate and acknowledge the achievement of the whole team (Armstrong 2000). Given the amount of project teamworking that is prevalent in organisations, using recognition programmes to promote the celebration of team successes would seem an obvious application.

Non-financial recognition for the whole team could complement a performance pay system that rewards individuals. When a team of employees achieves, the entire team needs to be recognised. If only the manager or highest performer is recognised, the team can lose motivation (Nelson 1994).

Who should do the recognising?

The author's 1998 survey found that 64 per cent of the recognition programmes reported were designed for the manager to recognise his or her people. Thirteen per cent of programmes were for colleagues to recognise each other and 23 per cent were for a variety of people.

Non-financial recognition programmes seem to break down into two main groups:

- those designed to support managers and encourage them to thank and genuinely recognise the great things their people do
- those designed for anyone in an organisation to recognise anyone else, like the Thames Water programme.

Which you choose will depend on the aim of the programme. An advantage of encouraging anyone to nominate people for awards is that it is likely to help build co-operation and teamworking. Some organisations particularly encourage people to recognise people in different departments but with whom they have regular contact – typically the internal customer.

The role of managers has changed and, with greater empowerment and flatter structures, they may miss some of the great things people do every day. So a programme allowing recognition from anyone can really help to 'catch people doing something right'. Some of the most powerful recognition comes when someone (or, more typically, a team) nominates his or her boss for recognition.

In addition to allowing everybody within the organisation to recognise people, some recognition programmes include stakeholders such as suppliers, contractors and customers. We are all familiar with customer service questionnaires in restaurants and hotels that ask if any member of staff is worthy of particular praise – hence the proliferation of name badges.

Some programmes include contractors and suppliers as potential recipients of recognition. This has to be considered carefully as their own organisation may have its own arrangements. But where there is a long-standing partnership between organisations, a co-ordinated approach can often be established.

Unlike BRAVO, which is purely a tool for managers, an Award for Excellence nomination may be made by anyone. Not only can British Airways employees be nominated, but also suppliers and contractors. The nomination may be made for an individual, a team or a 'station', which can be up to 50 people. There is no quota for these awards; the local representative will decide if the nomination is appropriate, based on his or her understanding of the standards in the company.

5

What and when should you recognise?

☑ What to recognise
☑ Immediate recognition
☑ Longer-term programmes

What to recognise

As opposed to a performance-related pay system or cash-based incentive plan, a recognition programme allows awards that are not dependent on achievement against a given target. Recognition programmes typically seek to recognise behaviours that fulfil overall values but are difficult, if not impossible, to record in terms of objectives – even if it were desirable to do so. It may be difficult to define precisely the behaviour that will be recognised, for example in the area of customer service (particularly given the emphasis on empowerment), but it might be captured in the phrase 'I'll know it when I see it.' This is not to say that a recognition programme should be unfocused, simply that it is not an incentive scheme.

The author's 1998 survey found that most organisations gave fairly loose guidelines on what should be recognised. Examples include:

- 'excellent customer service'
- 'something over and above the norm'
- 'innovation, improvements, suggestions'
- 'exceptional contribution and teamwork'.

In 1987 the First Interstate Bank of Oregon began a quality improvement programme that was based on recognising the good service employees already provided (Miller 1992). The bank found it to be so successful that the programme has been expanded across all the branches. The change was driven by a business need to change the bank's culture and differentiate itself in the market through providing excellent customer service. The initial emphasis was on finding a way to create new 'corporate heroes'. The belief was that these would be people that others would emulate. The initial definitions of good service came from employees rather than being issued from the corporate headquarters. A critical element of this approach was for the management to be clear about its goals. It needed to decide what was to be rewarded – service or sales and profitability. It had a belief that rewarding good service would ultimately translate into improved sales and profitability. Its aim was to 'create an environment where consideration, courtesy, teamwork, professionalism and mutual respect are values with real meaning'. The recognition programme is designed to reinforce an empowered culture where people are encouraged to think: 'If people do not buy in, when the going gets tough they will revert to policies and procedures.' The bank wanted to develop a corporate recognition programme. Employees, however, overwhelmingly said that they wanted the recognition effort to stop at the regional level.

A common approach is for the recognition programme to be used to recognise something 'over and above the call of duty'. However, an alternative approach is to use the programme simply to reinforce good norms of behaviour. For example, Boyle (1995) describes a programme introduced primarily to redress the balance between praise and criticism within the organisation and to improve communications. It was based on a system known as 'the 100 Club' which gave points for doing things that were always expected but often neglected, such as good attendance, punctuality, productivity and safety. The extrinsic value of the points was low, but the symbolic value was high, as they were a manifestation of the management's thanks.

British Airways gives guidelines on the sorts of things that might be recognised under the following headings:

- safety, security and health assurance
- customer service
- teamwork
- consistent high performance
- innovation and creativity
- global awareness
- good neighbourliness
- excellence in people management.

Health and safety issues may need to be taken into account in deciding what to recognise. An employee may do something great, for example showing a real sense of customer service, but does it conform to appropriate health and safety guidelines? It would give the wrong message if you recognise someone who puts himself at risk inappropriately. This can be a very difficult issue to manage

– if you empower people, then they will make their own decisions, but it can put the individual and the organisation at risk.

People working in some areas within an organisation may have more opportunities to display the sort of behaviours that are recognised, eg those in customer-facing roles. It is important to understand this and ensure that everyone can be recognised for the things they do, not just the high-profile functions. So if you want to use a recognition programme to help support great customer service, make sure you define it as applying to both internal and external customers – anyone in the value chain.

Recognition programmes can be introduced to reinforce quality initiatives. Cotton (1993) suggests that one of the reasons why quality circles are not maintained is because of a lack of recognition.

Programmes are more likely to aim to recognise effort, achievement, helping colleagues and performance than

Thames Water's recognition programme encourages anyone to nominate anyone else who 'truly reflects our values'. They have six stated values:

- success
- responsiveness
- professionalism
- honesty and integrity
- respect for others
- challenge and innovation.

The values are communicated on a single page, with each expanded into three to five bullet points.

competencies, although values (which to some extent may be elements of competencies) are often the basis for recognition. After all, an organisation that has made an effort to develop values will want to encourage people to recognise others who are clearly living these corporate values.

You can give guidelines on what should be recognised, but you cannot mandate them or give precise definitions. This inevitably means that some parts of the organisation will use a recognition programme more than others and recognise slightly different behaviours. You need to be able to live with this amount of difference. If you are to encourage a culture of recognition and thanks, you will also need to accept what might be seen as some inconsistency of application in your recognition programme.

Immediate recognition

As a general rule, companies formally reward employees on the basis of a 12-month cycle, typically related to the financial year. This emphasis on the annual cycle may come from the need for the organisation to manage its processes within a budgeting cycle, using a centrally administered process. But results and achievement do not fit neatly into this cycle which, in individual performance terms, is somewhat arbitrary. Reward and recognition programmes should reflect the reality of performance, not the administrative requirements (Wilson 1997).

Far more than other parts of the reward package, recognition programmes (particularly at the more informal end of the spectrum) allow immediate recognition of behaviour. Recognition should be both immediately after the event and spontaneous – the surprise adds to the power of the recognition.

To minimise the time lag between the accomplishment and the award, a decentralised approach is critical. Initial recognition must be immediate and, if you have other programmes to recognise people at a corporate level, then you still need to minimise the time period between the action and this more formal recognition.

Longer-term programmes

In the author's 1998 survey respondents said that their recognition schemes were designed to recognise people on the following timescales:

- any time: 46 per cent
- monthly: 20 per cent
- quarterly: 4 per cent
- annually: 30 per cent.

Typically, the more frequent awards were more informal and local, and the more infrequent were more formal and corporate. There may also be some duplication in that some companies reported a single programme that might have two levels, for example a monthly award that qualified the nominee for an annual award as well.

Although I advocate the value of local, informal, immediate recognition programmes, some organisations wish to have higher-profile and hence longer-term plans. These are discussed in Chapter 7.

6

What is the cost and effectiveness of recognition programmes?

☑ The effectiveness of recognition programmes
☑ The cost of recognition
☑ Budgeting for recognition programmes
  Central or local budgets – What elements do you need to
  budget for? – Tax and National Insurance

The effectiveness of recognition programmes

There is plenty of anecdotal evidence about the cost-effectiveness of recognition programmes. Pitts (1995) believes that recognition is very cost-effective. Boyle (1995) writes: 'When we say "thank you" to our employees, productivity goes through the ceiling. Recognition from within the organisation is more important to employees than money.' Boyle argues that a recognition programme that rewards mean performance reduces the dips in performance while slowly and incrementally building up the mean level of performance.

La Motta (1995) found that only about one-third of companies could answer a question on how effective their recognition programmes were. Even those answers were often vague. Friedson (1985) suggests that, although the benefits of recognition programmes may be difficult to quantify, so too are the deficits that result from the lack of this type of recognition. Even if the direct effect of recognition programmes cannot easily be measured, they are still able to send important messages about the value the organisation places on a particular behaviour (Flannery *et al* 1996). To that extent, recognition programmes can be effective in reinforcing corporate values and making the belief system more tangible.

Rank Xerox says that people felt better with recognition after they introduced a range of programmes. They undertake regular employee attitude surveys and found that the company's score on recognition is 8 per cent above the national norm.

The retail pub chain piloted the points approach with a sample group of pubs. Compared with a similar size control group, the pilot group sales growth increased by 3 per cent, profit by 9 per cent and the customer care score – measured by customer surveys – increased by 7 per cent. These numbers were very persuasive, and in January 1998 the scheme was launched across the rest of the branches.

One use for recognition programmes is as part of a suggestion scheme. Boyle (1995) provides data showing that, although rates are still considerably lower than in Japanese firms, US companies that have implemented a particular recognition programme had 10 times' the participation rate in their suggestion schemes as other US companies and double the adoption rate of suggestions.

Introducing a recognition programme can have a positive effect on employee relations. It may even act as a catalyst to change the behaviour and attitudes of management and labour. For example, a strongly unionised plant in the USA had a formally negotiated pay agreement. When a recognition programme using a joint management and employee group was introduced, there was a high degree of scepticism from unionised employees who had only ever seen gains through 'hard fought negotiations'. They were suspicious of a hidden agenda. However, it was highly successful in improving productivity. Whereas the management would have had considerable difficulties in trying to introduce such improvements through a negotiated pay-based mechanism, by introducing a non-financial recognition programme outside the pay arena, and ensuring it was entirely in addition to other elements, considerable benefits were gained (Boyle 1995). These benefits came both from the recognition programme itself and, more indirectly, from the improvement in labour–management relations that the programme engendered.

The cost of recognition

A survey of over 100 companies in the USA found that only four companies could give any indication of the costs of their programmes (La Motta 1995). Yet cost is a significant difference between pay systems and recognition programmes. Whereas the former can amount to up to 65 per cent of an organisation's costs, the latter are relatively cheap to run. Friedson (1985) suggests as a rule of thumb that corporations should budget between 0.5 and 1 per cent of their payroll to fund award programmes, although he also says that much of that money is often left unspent.

A very informal recognition programme can cost almost nothing. Maynard (1997) quotes the CEO of a US food company, which operates a number of recognition award programmes, who says that 'though there may be economic restraints on what we pay them, there are no restraints on the recognition we give them'.

Seventy-four per cent of the respondents to the author's 1998 survey agreed with the statement that 'the recognition programmes that we operate are very good value for money.' The companies' statement about what they spent on such programmes suggest that they typically cost less than 0.5 per cent of payroll.

Budgeting for recognition programmes

Even where no corporately sponsored programmes exist, it is common to find pockets of good recognition practice within organisations. Managers who understand the value of such an approach often find a way to fund some informal local recognition, such as sending a successful team out to dinner, or presenting someone with a case of wine. It is important that the introduction of a broader programme does not stifle these initiatives – rather it should learn from and capitalise on them. Harvey-Jones (1994) believes that 'every manager should have a small "float" to enable him to produce such forms of recognition in whatever seems the most appropriate way.'

Central or local budgets

Where an informal non-cash award programme is being established, should it be budgeted from within each department or centrally? There is a strong argument for a central budget initially to get it off the ground. Furthermore, since you cannot limit recognition to a quota, some departments will inevitably use a recognition programme more than others. A local budget can lead to recognition being given solely to meet a quota or budget rather than because of a genuine desire to recognise something great someone has done.

Initially the budget for the British Airways schemes was held centrally so that a manager did not have to consider the costs against his own budget. Subsequently, although the budget is still held centrally, the total costs of the schemes are recharged out at a very high divisional level that should still not influence the managers making the recognition.

What elements do you need to budget for?

- initial publicity and launch materials – posters, guidelines, intranet
- cost of the awards themselves
- certificates or trophies
- celebration events – catering, venue, invitations, etc
- tax and National Insurance on awards.

Tax and National Insurance

A potential risk of local arrangements is that any tax or National Insurance liability is not correctly accounted for. It may be that benefits are being given to employees on which tax and NI are due. By capturing the existing range of programmes you can at least manage this risk.

It is normal practice for the employer to settle any employee tax and NI arising from a recognition award. It is therefore important to discuss this with your tax department or advisors. The enthusiasm and goodwill generated by a non-financial award is immediately damaged, even destroyed, if the employee suddenly finds himself taxed on the benefit.

It is also important to make the point to employees that the tax is being paid by the organisation.

> Thames Water gives a cheque for £1,000 (and certificate) to its VIP winners. Since it pays any taxes due, the individual is presented with a cheque that is his or hers to spend freely.

How do you get started?

Defining objectives and successful outcomes

Organisations need to be clear about their reasons for introducing a recognition programme and ensure that it fits the company culture and values. Like any other HR strategy, a recognition programme will not be effective if it is simply grafted on to the existing processes. Before introducing a new programme, carefully consider what it is trying to achieve and the context within which it will be introduced.

A programme will not work in isolation with a disgruntled or demotivated workforce; it has to be part of a whole culture of valuing people (Syedain 1995). La Motta (1995) is critical of some recognition programmes that are not part of a cultural change and simply allow managers smugly to believe that people are genuinely recognised because of the programmes that are run.

Thames Water gives the purpose of its Values in Practice (VIP) recognition scheme as:

- to identify the unsung heroes of the organisation, recognise them as role models and celebrate their success
- to recognise and celebrate exceptional achievements that demonstrate our company values
- anyone can nominate any member of Thames Water group of companies who in their daily activities truly reflect our values.

The author's 1998 survey found the top four reasons for introducing a recognition programme were:

- to recognise performance 'above and beyond'
- to improve customer service
- to recognise achievement
- to support line managers.

British Airways went through considerable change in the late 1980s. One of the most significant cultural changes it faced was to move from a company that was engineering-based and operationally focused to one that was service-based and customer-focused. An important part of the change was a customer care training programme introduced at that time called 'Putting People First'. Part of the change process was the need to recognise what excellent customer service looked like. To reinforce the emphasis on customer care, a recognition programme was launched in 1988 for customer-facing staff – eg cabin staff – called 'Awards for Excellence'. The aim of this programme was to recognise examples of excellent customer care.

The author worked with a public-sector organisation to review and relaunch its recognition programme. The purpose of the relaunched programme was defined as 'to recognise the behaviour of people in providing excellent customer service and/or support for colleagues over and above the norms of their job'.

Employee and customer surveys

Attitude/satisfaction surveys of employees and customers can be both a stimulus to introduce a recognition programme and the means of identifying its success.

The retail pub chain regularly undertook 'culture surveys' that, in 1996, identified two particular problem areas. One was what was seen as poor communications with staff and poor recognition of people. The catering industry also suffers from very high staff turnover. In bringing these issues together the HR function considered the introduction of a voucher-based reward and recognition system to address these issues.

> British Airways undertook research to analyse customer and employee attitudes and satisfaction levels. Recognition programmes were extended from the customer-facing staff as a result of this research in 1993.

If you introduce a recognition programme based on such a survey, then you could aim to improve the 'recognition score' as a result. Exit or termination interviews are also a valuable source of information. Again, they may be used to help identify if there is a lack of recognition in the organisation as well as to track changes post implementation.

A FTSE-100 business introduced five different recognition programmes, ranging from the very informal to the formal and corporate-wide, to improve the recognition culture in the business. In its latest attitude survey (reported in the author's 1998 survey), it reported that 82 per cent of people agreed that 'I am thanked by my manager for a job well done.' And 73 per cent agreed that 'I am satisfied with the recognition I receive from my manager for doing my job well.' These are both high positive scores.

It is not recommended that you measure success simply by the numbers of recognition awards used. You need to get underneath this and look for changes in attitudes or behaviours.

Review what's there

Even if no recognition programmes have been formally implemented, it is common to find a range of existing recognition practices within the organisation. This is particularly likely in a decentralised organisation. Before developing a completely new recognition programme, try to find out what people are already doing. Work with them to develop a programme that can be used more widely.

> Some departments in British Airways already had their own recognition programmes operating at varying levels of success and funded within their budgets. For example, Customer Service had Bronze, Silver and Gold lapel pins that were awarded for different levels of customer service. Such programmes typically fill a perceived gap in the corporate programmes. These programmes were each different and were owned by each department. There was no attempt by HR to stifle these local initiatives nor take them over as centralised processes; rather they are referred to, in general terms, in the management guide.

Maximising the effectiveness of recognition

Designing and developing effective communications and publicity are critical to maximise the effectiveness of recognition programmes. This needs to be considered from a number of angles.

Publicise/launch the whole programme

If a recognition programme is designed just to encourage managers to thank and recognise people fairly informally, then you may not wish to communicate the scheme outside the manager group. Otherwise, as Gryna (1992) advocates, publicity is the key to launching and continuing a successful recognition programme. One way to begin this process, he suggests, is to encourage employee participation when designing the programme. The longer that a reward is used, the more difficult it is to maintain employee enthusiasm, therefore significant emphasis must be placed on continued publicity. Materials used to launch the programme need to be high quality and look professional.

> The retail pub chain took particular care in the quality of the materials, the catalogue, etc, and the communications, recognising that the medium is the message; the scheme was launched with a series of road shows to ensure that everyone understood it. Each of the many thousands of employees got a copy of the catalogue. They each received a monthly statement showing their points balance. The quality of the materials was seen as key to the success of the scheme. It reflected the sort of quality associated with customers, the message being: employees are important and we have taken as much care with this scheme as we would have taken with something for one of our external customers.

Brief managers or others involved

The programme(s) may need to be built into, for example, management training and induction programmes.

> British Airways has a well-designed, simple managers' briefing pack that explains what recognition is about and how it should be done, and that includes an illustrated list of awards and the process of getting them. For example, it gives the following guideline:
>
> **What is recognition?**
> Very simply, recognition is saying 'thank you' to show your appreciation for a job well done. It shows people that we value them and their contribution to the success of British Airways.

There are many ways to thank someone, but how you give recognition is almost as important as what you give. Remember:

- Everyone needs to feel appreciated – don't assume they know they are doing a good job.
- Say 'thank you' as soon after the event as possible.
- Celebrate the behaviours and actions you want to encourage.
- However you choose to say thank you, make it meaningful for that person.
- Don't recognise for the sake of it – or because someone may feel 'left out'.

The actual recognition of individuals

You will need to give guidance to people on how to recognise people.

Thames Water has around 50 nominations per quarter for its VIP recognition scheme. Each individual nominated receives a letter personally signed by the CEO, informing them of who has nominated them and for what. This reflects back what they did and informs them of the next stage. The text may be something like this:

I am writing to say how pleased I am that John Smith has nominated you for the September Values in Practice Award. Your nomination was for the way you...Many congratulations on your achievements. My colleagues in the Executive Management Team and I are looking forward to announcing the winner, who will receive the award in September. Meanwhile, many thanks for this outstanding demonstration of our values.

The person nominating will also get a personal letter from the CEO, such as:

I was delighted to receive your nomination of Sally Jones for a Values In Practice Award. From all the nominations we receive, my colleagues in the Executive Management Team and I will choose a winner for September. One of the Values in Practice team may contact you for more information if we need to clarify anything about your nomination. In the meantime, thank you for taking the time to make the nomination, and for recognising the achievements of your colleague.

Publicise formal programme winners

This is so that what the winners have done can be shared throughout the organisation as role models. The choice of media will depend on your normal channels, but company newspapers or intranet are common. Real stories of what real people have done can be very positive and something that colleagues can identify with.

Both British Airways and Thames Water publicise people recognised in their company-wide magazines.

Building a series of recognition programmes over different timescales

When people think of recognition programmes it is often the more formal 'employee of the year' type schemes that come to mind. Some organisations' reaction to a lack of thanks and appreciation is to bureaucratise this into an HR-driven corporate programme. It is fairly easy to design a single high-profile company-wide scheme that will allow the CEO to mouth some platitudes on people being our greatest asset at a corporate bean feast.

However, a highly rules-based recognition programme is more likely to constrain than to encourage true recognition. Hertzberg believes that recognition of individual achievement is unlikely to flourish in a bureaucratic situation. The framework of rules and regulations may limit the opportunities to display individual achievement as well as the opportunity to recognise it.

The local informal approach, which is open-ended and which people can more easily relate to, is likely to be more effective than the large corporate event, particularly as there are normally a pre-stated number of 'winners' permissible at corporate events. So the place to start is not with the top-down corporate programme, but the informal local programmes. Try to drive the genuine recognition of people in an immediate, spontaneous way through providing guidance and access to some suitable awards. A new informal programme will probably need to 'bed down' over a couple of years before any additional programmes can be introduced. But talk to line managers and others in the organisation and review how it is doing and if there is a place for a more formal arrangement in addition to the informal programme.

You may wish to add a second level that has as its starting point all of those people recognised informally. Depending on the informality of the local programme, you may wish to add a slightly higher-value recognition opportunity that requires some sort of written statement about the action deserving recognition, etc. This may go to a central point or a local co-ordinator to note or authorise its suitability for a higher-value award.

From the informal programme you can input nominations to a more formal recognition event to be held quarterly, half-yearly or annually. I favour the quarterly or half-yearly approach, as an annual recognition programme can mean a very long time between the action and the formal award. You will also need to consider carefully the level of profile, celebration and publicity of this more formal recognition event.

The author's 1998 survey found that the 61 participating major UK companies with recognition programmes had 116 programmes between them. This is illustrated in the table below. The survey also showed that the majority (65 per cent) of recognition programmes are at the informal end of the continuum.

Where there is more than one programme they are often designed for different groups, such as sales or customer services as opposed to corporate functions. Some companies

Number of recognition programmes	Number of organisations	
	Number	%
1	36	59
2	10	16
3	8	13
4	0	0
5	6	10
6	1	2
Total	61	100

design programmes that are solely for team rather than individual nomination. These are frequently very similar to the individual programme. Where there are a number of programmes that are common across the company, they are usually linked so that people recognised informally may go on to become nominees on the more formal programme.

The British Airways BRAVO programme is an example of how the approach to recognition can span this continuum. The guidelines to managers explain the range of recognition responses that are appropriate, depending on the behaviour or activity to be recognised:

- an excellent day-to-day job – written or oral commendation
- Extra Contribution – a BRAVO award: a choice of gifts (typically under £50 in value) to be presented to the individual or sent to his or her home address
- Special Contribution – an Award for Excellence (AfE): a more formal and public 'thank you', a significant presentation with a gift value of around £200 and a certificate signed by the CEO
- Exceptional Contribution – chosen quarterly from all of the successful AfEs: winners are invited to a luxury weekend break abroad hosted by a Director and presented with a signed certificate by the chairman.

Regular review

Even if a recognition programme is seen to be effective, like any other HR programme it needs to be periodically reviewed to keep it effective – at least every two years. ICL used to provide a range of gifts under an Olympic-type programme – gold, silver and bronze. However, after a project team conducted employee research it was found that people preferred a choice of gift from a catalogue. Reacting to this employee feedback the company relaunched its recognition programme using a catalogue called 'Excellence Collection'.

Nelson (1997) suggests that indicators of a need to review a recognition programme are:

- loss of excitement so that no one talks about the programme
- dwindling participation
- jokes and complaints about it rather than it being a source of pride.

The programme can be rejuvenated in many different ways, such as:

- celebrating say the 500th award
- changing the choice of awards
- adding a special category such as team award
- changing the group who may select nominees for a corporate award
- linking the programme to other initiatives, such as suggestion schemes.

British Airways' 'Award for Excellence' programme had been operating for customer-facing staff since 1988, but by 1994 nominations were dropping and the second level of the award was being cancelled. It was declining in use; it was clearly unsupported and was not being communicated. It was decided to revamp the programme, making it available across the whole company, including overseas operations. The materials were redesigned and new criteria were agreed.

Golden rules

- Consider carefully the impact and relationship between the new recognition programme(s) and existing HR programmes, such as reward, performance management and training.
- Build on existing informal programmes that some line managers may already be running.
- Recognition should be immediately after the event, it should be sincere and should match the award to the person and the achievement.
- Encourage recognition to be delivered in an open and public way.
- Do not try to limit recognition to a budget or a quota.
- Do not try to measure the success of a programme simply by the number of awards made.
- Introduce low-key informal line-manager-based programmes before bringing in any more formal programmes.
- Issue support and guidelines to managers, but do not use specific goals or measurable objectives as the criteria for awards.
- Provide budget for a range of relatively low-value non-cash awards that can be matched to the person and the achievement.
- Use peer groups rather than senior managers to make decisions on those to receive awards from a number of nominations.
- Monitor the programmes and expect to refresh them regularly.

Action plans - checklist

- Review rationale for considering a recognition programme – survey evidence, exit interviews, management views, etc.
- Research – visit other organisations with recognition programmes, read about them – look at the reference section at the back of this book.
- Discuss outline ideas with key stakeholders in the organisation; agree concept in principle.
- Form a design and implementation project team.
- Define aims of the scheme – medium-term aims and overall plans; establish what success indicators will be.
- Consider how you will explain the relationship between the recognition programme and other HR programmes, particularly reward.
- Establish an outline budget.
- Develop a scheme structure – who can recognise who, level of awards, etc.
- Determine how to provide awards – do it yourself or outsource the process?
- Agree proposals with the senior team as appropriate – timing, budget, etc.
- Develop programme guidelines and launch publicity.
- Launch.
- Review regularly; monitor both programme and success indicators.

Good luck for a successful recognition programme!

References

ARMSTRONG M. (1996) *Employee Reward*. London, IPD.

ARMSTRONG M. (2000) *Rewarding Teams*. London, IPD.

BLANCHARD K. *and* JOHNSON S. (1993) *The One-Minute Manager*. London, HarperCollins.

BOYLE D. C. (1995) *Secrets of a Successful Employee Recognition System*. Portland, Oregon, Productivity Press.

BROOKS S. S. (1994) 'Noncash ways to compensate employees'. *HR Magazine*. Vol. 39, No. 4, April. pp38–44.

BRYANT S. (1994) 'Say it with flowers'. *Human Resources*. Summer. pp120–125.

CARNEGIE D. (1936) *How to Win Friends and Influence People*. New York, Simon & Schuster.

CAUDRON S. (1995) 'The top 20 ways to motivate employees'. *Industry Week*. Vol. 244, No. 7, 3 April. pp12–16.

CBI/HAY (1995) 'Trends in pay and benefits systems'. Survey results.

CLINE B. (1997) 'Rewarding employees through non-monetary compensation'. *Human Resource Professional*. August/September. pp19–23.

COTTON L. J. (1993) *Employee Involvement*. Newbury Park, California, Sage.

FLANNERY T. P., HOFRICHTER D. A. *and* PLATTEN P. E. (1996) *People, Performance and Pay*. New York, The Free Press.

FREIBERG K. *and* FREIBERG J. (1996) *Nuts! Southwest Airlines'*

Crazy Recipe for Business and Personal Success. Marietta, Georgia, Bard Press.

FRIEDSON A. S. (1985) 'Special award programs: compensating excellence'. *Personnel Administrator*. September. pp105–114.

GODDARD R. W. (1987) 'Well Done!'. *Management World*. Vol. 16, No. 6, November–December. pp14–16.

GRYNA D. (1992) 'Celebrating success'. *Managing Service Quality*. September. pp329–333.

HALE R. E. *and* MAEHLING R. F. (1993) *Recognition Redefined*. Exeter, New Hampshire, Monochrome Press.

HARVEY-JONES J. (1994) *All Together Now*. London, Heinemann.

HEMSATH D. *and* YERKES L. (1997) *301 Ways to Have Fun at Work*. San Francisco, California, Berrett-Koehler.

HERTZBERG F. (1968) *Work and the Nature of Man*. London, Granada.

HERTZBERG F., MAUSNER B. *and* SNYDERMAN B. B. (1959) *The Motivation to Work*. New York, John Wiley & Sons.

JOHNSON R. *and* REDMOND D. (1998) *The Art of Empowerment*. London, Financial Times Pitman Publishing.

JOINSON C. (1996) 'Reward your best employees'. *HR Magazine*. April. pp49–55.

KLUBNIK J. P. (1995) *Rewarding and Recognizing Employees*. New York, Irwin.

LA MOTTA T. (1995) *Recognition – the Quality Way*. New York, Quality Resources.

LEGGE K. (1995) *Human Resource Management*. London, Macmillan.

LYONS L. (2000) 'Management is dead...'. *People Management*. 26 October. pp60–64.

MANAGING CUSTOMER SERVICE (1998) 'Exclusive MCS

Survey: latest benchmarks for pay, rewards and recognition'. February.

MASLOW A. H. (1970) *Motivation and Personality*. New York, Harper & Row.

MAYNARD R. (1997) 'How to motivate low-wage workers'. *Nation's Business*. May.

MILLER B. W. (1992) 'Banking on good service'. *Managing Service Quality*. November. pp399–401.

NELSON B. (1994) *1001 Ways to Reward Employees*. New York, Workman Publishing.

NELSON B. (1996) 'Dump the cash, load on the praise'. *Personnel Journal*. July. pp65–70.

NELSON B. (1997) 'Low-cost ways to energize employees'. *HR Magazine*. Vol. 42, No. 12, December. pp45–48.

PFEFFER J. (1998) 'Six dangerous myths about pay'. *Harvard Business Review*. May–June. pp109–119.

PITTS C. (1995) *Motivating Your Organisation*. Maidenhead, McGraw-Hill.

ROFFEY PARK MANAGEMENT INSTITUTE (1999) *The Management Agenda*.

ROSE M. (2000) 'Performance targets'. *People Management*. 23 November. pp44–45.

STEERS R. M. *and* PORTER L. W. (1991) *Motivation and Work Behavior*. New York, McGraw-Hill.

SYEDAIN H. (1995) 'The rewards of recognition'. *Management Today*. May. pp72–74.

TROY K. (1993) 'Recognize quality achievement with noncash awards'. *Personnel Journal*. October. pp111–117.

TULGAN B. (1996) *Managing Generation X*. Oxford, Capstone.

TYSON S. (1995) *Human Resource Strategy*. London, Pitman.

WILSON S. Y. (1997) 'When is compensation not enough'. *Compensation and Benefits Review*. Vol. 29, No. 1. pp59–64.

With over 100,000 members, the **Chartered Institute of Personnel and Development** is the largest organisation in Europe dealing with the management and development of people. The CIPD operates its own publishing unit, producing books and research reports for human resource practitioners, students, and general managers charged with people management responsibilities.

Currently there are over 150 titles, covering the full range of personnel and development issues. The books have been commissioned from leading experts in the field and are packed with the latest information and guidance to best practice.

For free copies of the CIPD Books Catalogue, please contact the publishing department:
Tel: 020 8263 3387
Fax: 020 8263 3850
E-mail: *publish@cipd.co.uk*
Web: *www.cipd.co.uk*

Orders for books should be sent direct to:
Plymbridge Distributors
Estover
Plymouth
Devon PL6 7PY
Tel: +44 (0) 1752 202301
Fax: +44 (0) 1752 202333
E-mail: orders@plymbridge.com

Bullying and Sexual Harassment

by

Tina Stephens

Most organisations are aware of the serious legal implications of allowing bullying or sexual harassment to flourish in the workplace. Morale can be affected if management does not act, with consequences for productivity and effectiveness. Up to date and to the point, this guide will show how to:

- write, establish and develop a formal policy for dealing with both bullying and sexual harassment
- understand and communicate the influence of bullying and harassment on absenteeism, productivity and reputation
- establish formal and informal complaints procedures
- train managers to recognise problems early and raise awareness.

1999   96 pages   ISBN 0 85292 825 4   **£9.99**

Career Development

by

Tricia Jackson

How do HR practitioners manage and develop the careers of their staff in today's fast-moving and rapidly changing world of work? What is a career, when employees change jobs more frequently than ever before and the concept of 'the job for life' has apparently withered and died? This Good Practice guide will help the reader understand and use the competencies required for good career development, including negotiation and communication, and coaching and performance appraisal.

2000   112 pages   ISBN 0 85292 851 3   £9.99

Creating a Staff Handbook

by

Clare Hogg

The staff handbook is the organisation's bible. It is the first place employees will look for essential information on the practices and procedures of their workplace. How do you make sure the staff handbook is the definitive source of information it should be? This invaluable guide shows:

- how to produce, maintain and revise a staff handbook
- examples from staff handbooks
- the legal aspects and communication issues.

1999   112 pages   ISBN 0 85292 822 X   **£9.99**

Drugs and Alcohol Policies

by

Tricia Jackson

This guide shows how to put alcohol and drugs policies into practice and how to make them really work. *Drugs and Alcohol Policies*:

- provides help on how to write alcohol and drugs policies
- considers the health and safety aspects of alcohol and drug abuse
- tackles related problems such as absenteeism, competence and relationships at work
- explains employers' rights and obligations under UK law.

1999   112 pages   ISBN 0 85292 811 4   **£9.99**

Handling Grievances

by

Tricia Jackson

This book provides the essential tools and techniques for handling grievances. It explains in detail how to:

- introduce (or enhance) a comprehensive grievance procedure
- avoid damaging disputes and unnecessary legal claims
- conduct a professional grievance interview
- respond effectively to employee worries and complaints.

2000   104 pages   ISBN 0 85292 885 8   **£9.99**